Ann and Paul Brahms of Portland, Maine, are two dog breeders dedicated to the belief that in training puppies a lot of love, socialization, and discipline goes a long way.

Along with breeding and showing their own animals, the Brahms taught obedience and breed handling classes for several years.

They have bred several varieties of dogs over the past two decades. All of the puppies that they have placed in homes have had the benefit of considerable human contact. It is their contention that puppies are capable of learning as early as 49 days old. They have taught every puppy in their litters to obey the commands Sit, Stand, Down, and No Bite before they were placed in their new homes.

# PUPPY ED.

## Training Your Dog at an Early Age

### by
### Ann and Paul Brahms
### Illustrated by Paul Brahms, Jr.

**BALLANTINE BOOKS • NEW YORK**

ISBN 0-345-33512-0

Photographs courtesy of Guy Gannett Publishing Company

This edition published by arrangement with Brahms Publishing Company

Manufactured in United States of America

First Ballantine Books Edition: November 1986

We wish to dedicate this book to our good friend

Frances Tuck

for her tireless efforts to train hundreds of dog owners throughout the years and for the stiff, but friendly, competition in the obedience ring. Frances has been and will always be an inspiration to us.

And in memory of
Onyx, Tier, Fonzie, and Jody.

# Acknowledgements

With love and appreciation we would like to thank our family and friends for their support and patience as we undertook this endeavor.

A very special word of thanks goes to the following people:

To our son Paul for using his artistic talents in designing both the front and back covers and for illustrating some of the key points we tried to make.

Ann's brother Dana W. Allen for his grammatical expertise while we were in the early stages of writing this book.

To Jane and Bill Brahms, Haddonfield, New Jersey, who edited the final work and who were always a source of encouragement.

# Contents

# Introduction

Puppies are not born knowing all the social graces. They must be taught good manners, the same as children.

The purpose of this book is to share with you the methods of training puppies that we have learned over the years. They have worked well with our puppies beginning at seven weeks of age. If carried out correctly and consistently, they should work well with yours.

By following these methods, your puppy can be taught good habits before it develops bad ones on its own.

# Vocabulary

It has been our experience that anyone who wishes to succeed in training a puppy to be obedient must use a specific vocabulary and adhere to it.

Whenever we train a puppy, a small group of words is used as one means of communicating with the dog. These key words may be few; however, they play a major role in the dog's training and control. In order to avoid confusing the puppy, these words are never substituted for other words.

Throughout this book, these key words are listed at the beginning of each lesson, indicating that they will be used for that specific exercise.

# Vocabulary

To acquaint the reader beforehand, the vocabulary that we use to communicate with our dogs is divided into the following categories on the next few pages: commands, praise, reassurance, displeasure, release.

## Commands

To command simply means to give an order. When we give a command to a dog, we use the fewest words possible. We never ask the dog to obey. If a command is spoken correctly, a firm tone of voice will communicate that an immediate response is expected. A dog that responds to the first command is well trained. Never, under any conditions, should it be necessary to repeat an order. Repetition of a command teaches a puppy that it can disregard authority. Disobedience will be the end result.

The commands we use are:

| | |
|---|---|
| COME | OFF |
| OUT | STAND |
| NO | SIT |
| LET'S GO | INSIDE |

BACK NO BITE
DOWN STAY
OUTSIDE

## Praise

Praising a dog communicates approval of its actions. Praise is the only reward we give our dogs, so it is carried out with a great deal of petting and excited enthusiasm in a pleased tone of voice. Other words of praise can be substituted, however, the phrase we generally use is:

GOOD DOG! (spoken with much
enthusiasm)

## Reassurance

Reassurance is a means of putting the puppy at ease or encouraging it. The word we use to accomplish this with our dogs is:

EASY! (spoken in a calm, gentle tone of
voice)

## Displeasure

To let our dogs know that we are displeased
with their behavior, we use the words:

SHAME!

NO!

(spoken always in a stern tone of voice)

## Release

To release a dog from a command, we use the
word:

OK (in a happy, enthusiastic tone of
voice)

# Housebreaking A Puppy

**Key words:** SHAME
OUTSIDE
GOOD DOG
INSIDE

In the early stages of their development, young puppies generally need to relieve themselves several times a day. More control over body elimination will come as the puppy grows older, if it is in good health and has had proper, consistent training. Until that time (assuming one is not paper training a dog), it may be helpful to realize beforehand that housebreaking a puppy often requires many trips outside, regardless of weather conditions.

If a puppy is to live in the house and be considered a member of the family, **it should be housebroken as soon as possible**—for obvious reasons.

The method we use to housebreak our puppies is as follows:

The puppy is always taken outside after it has eaten, had a lot of water, played for any length of time, before bed and when it wakes up. It is evident from this that housebreaking can be a time-consuming procedure, however, a necessary one. Taking the puppy outside after any of the occasions just mentioned helps the dog to better understand where it is to go to eliminate. This also reduces the number of mistakes the dog will have to be disciplined for by seeking relief in the house. As the puppy is taken out of the house, the word OUTSIDE is spoken once and only once in a firm tone of voice.

Outdoors, someone always stays with the puppy to be certain it does eliminate. Patience is essential, for puppies often move their bowels twice before they are finished.

As soon as elimination has taken place, the puppy is praised by saying the phrase GOOD DOG in a pleased tone of voice. As the puppy is returned to the house, the word INSIDE is spoken. By going indoors right away, the puppy learns that as soon as it seeks relief, it can go inside—this seldom displeases any dog!

In the house, the puppy is confined to an area that is most accessible to the outside; the shorter the distance to travel, the better.

Until the puppy understands better, it will make mistakes at times by relieving itself on the floor. The manner in which the puppy is disciplined for this is extremely important. **The puppy is never called to come for a correction.** Someone always goes to the puppy or takes it to the spot where the error was made. **Calling a dog should always be a happy experience.**

Never carry out a correction by hitting the puppy, nor punish it by rubbing its nose in a mistake. Also, never use a newspaper to threaten or hit a puppy.

Correction is done by saying the word SHAME in a stern tone of voice. This word is all the discipline necessary to show a puppy that it has done something wrong.

After the dog has been properly shamed— that is, corrected—it is taken outside immediately. The handler then says the word OUTSIDE while the dog is being taken out.

A puppy will often seek relief near an area where it has previously eliminated. If a puppy is taken to a familiar place, chances are good that it will eliminate more quickly. This helps to reduce the amount of time spent outside, and it's an added benefit if the weather is poor. Feeding the puppy at the same time of day every day will help the dog to develop regular habits of elimination.

This section on housebreaking would not be complete if we failed to mention the safety of the dog. If the area where the puppy is taken to eliminate is not fenced in, use a collar and leash to protect the animal.

Patience and consistency are the keys to successfully housebreaking a puppy.

# Chewing
# and Nibbling

**Key words:** NO BITE
OUT
GOOD DOG

**Equipment:** Hard rubber dog toys/rawhide bone

**M**ost puppies love to chew and nibble on just about anything. They usually go after objects that are on the floor or close to it within their reach—shoes, socks, table legs, chair legs, and so on. Some puppies enjoy chewing on the padding in sofas, chairs, and mattresses. We must not forget to mention some really enjoyable treats: fingers and toes!

The method we use to correct a puppy that

chews or nibbles on the wrong thing is as follows:

First, we buy a supply of dog toys and a bone. These are left on the floor all the time so that the puppy has access to them. The toys we use are made of hard rubber, which we find quite durable; the bone is made of rawhide.

When the puppy begins to chew or nibble on a person, it is immediately corrected by being told NO BITE / OUT in a stern tone of voice. (This is said once and only once!) Next, the puppy is grasped by the scruff of the neck and given a few firm shakes to stop it from continuing this bad behavior. As soon as the puppy stops it is praised by saying GOOD DOG in a pleased tone of voice.

When experiencing this correction for the first time some puppies will respond by turning in the direction of the trainer's hand which was used to give the correction and attempt to bite at it. If this happens the correction should be repeated immediately. This reaction is understandable in that it is the method most puppies use to react to its litter mates when they display excessive aggression.

To be effective, **this procedure must be carried out in the same manner every time the puppy begins to chew or nibble on someone until it stops.** Never allow a puppy to get away with this bad habit because later it could turn into a dangerous situation. It also hurts!

This method of correction is also used when the puppy chews or nibbles on objects. This time, however, someone must go to the puppy to correct it. **Remember, calling a dog should always be a happy occasion.**

As soon as the puppy is corrected, give it a dog toy or bone to play with. The puppy understands from this what is allowed. At this time, praise the puppy by saying GOOD DOG in a pleased tone of voice. This method of puppy training, like all others, must be carried out consistently to be effective.

It may be of interest to learn how we came about using the scruff-of-the-neck correction method described earlier in this section. We discovered it by observing Tier, our beloved female Doberman Pinscher. This was the method she used to correct her puppies when they chewed or nibbled on her. First, Tier would growl a warning to let the puppy know that she was not at all pleased with its actions. Next, she would pick up the puppy by the scruff of its neck with her mouth. She would lift it off the floor and proceed to shake it—not too gently—until she felt the puppy had learned a lesson. Once she felt the discipline was sufficient, she would release the puppy and let it drop to the floor.

## Chewing and Nibbling

This gentle, loving Doberman was always consistent in training her puppies until they understood that chewing and nibbling on their mother was not allowed. It always worked for her, as it has for us ever since.

# Aggressive
# Behavior

**Key words:** NO
GOOD DOG

There's always a puppy here and there that decides it will create a fuss about someone petting it or handling its possessions—food or toys, for example—while it is eating or chewing. Usually a puppy that protests does so by growling. However, some try to nip and bite.

Never, under any circumstances, should any puppy be allowed to get away with such potentially dangerous behavior. This is especially important when the safety of children is at stake. Our puppies are taught from the start that they must always tolerate anyone petting them and touching whatever they are eating or chewing, **no matter what!**

The method we use to prevent this form of aggressive behavior from developing is as follows:

The puppy is petted often while at the same time its possessions are being touched. Each member of the family takes a turn doing this, as do friends when they come to visit. To always be on the safe side, this procedure is repeated occasionally throughout the life of the dog.

If a puppy shows aggression of any kind, it is immediately and sternly told NO, spoken once and only once! The puppy is then grasped by the scruff of its neck and shaken firmly to stop this aggressive act. Once the puppy stops, it is told GOOD DOG in a pleased tone of voice.

In order for this method of correction to be effective, it must be repeated the same way every time the puppy shows any kind of aggression.

Brahms Selten Tier gently taking a treat from the hand of Master David Brahms both three years of age.

**Off the furniture?**
**Tier and Treu caught in the act.**

# Keeping A Puppy Off Furniture

**Key words:** OFF
GOOD DOG

As a rule, most people love to cuddle a puppy. This is as it should be. However, where the cuddling is done makes a big difference. We get down on the floor to socialize with our dogs. We learned the hard way that if socializing takes place on a sofa, chair or bed, a puppy usually will make it a favorite resting place.

In the past, we have had to replace costly furniture because of pets jumping up and sleeping there. Toenails damaged the cushions;

dog hairs and odors clung steadfastly from constant use. In the end, the furniture was ruined and had to be thrown away. All this could have been avoided if we had taken the time then to teach our puppies that they were not allowed to get on the furniture.

Here's the method we now follow to prevent this bad habit from getting started:

Never encourage, coax or put a puppy on any furniture!

If a puppy attempts to jump or climb onto anything that is not allowed, go immediately to the puppy and say the word OFF in a stern tone of voice spoken once and only once. The puppy is then placed back on the floor at which time the phrase GOOD DOG is said in a pleased tone of voice.

Few puppies ever learn from the first lesson. This procedure is carried out in the same way each time a puppy attempts to get on furniture.

If the puppy is kept in a room that is not under supervision and you suspect that it is getting onto furniture, cover the furniture with books or any objects that will make it difficult for the puppy to climb on. This should be enough to discourage the dog when there's no one around to correct the situation.

# Jumping on People

**Key words:** NO
OFF
GOOD DOG

It has been our experience that it is far easier to teach a puppy that it is not allowed to jump on people than it is to put up with the constant aggravation of one that does.

Our puppies are taught early that they are not permitted to jump on people. We teach them early because they're Doberman Pinschers and when full grown they're rather large as well as strong. It wouldn't take much effort for one of them to unintentionally knock someone down by jumping up.

Regardless of the size and strength of the dog, we feel that jumping up is a most annoying bad habit. Muddy paw prints soil good clothing and hosiery is easily ruined by the dog's toenails; the nails can also hurt if raked across the skin.

We use two different methods to correct a puppy that jumps up on people. The first one is the procedure most frequently used. The second is carried out if we have a problem with a puppy that insists on jumping up even after it knows otherwise.

(1) When a puppy jumps up on someone, it is immediately told NO / OFF, spoken just once in a stern tone of voice! The puppy is then lifted off the person by its two front paws and gently placed on the floor and praised with GOOD DOG! This procedure is repeated the same way every time the puppy jumps up—until it understands that this behavior is not allowed.

(2) If, after a reasonable length of time, the puppy does not respond to the first method of correction, it is corrected after it jumps up by again saying NO / OFF, spoken just once in a stern tone of voice! The trainer then holds the puppies two front paws, squeezing lightly until the puppy tires of

this position. It is then returned gently to the floor and told GOOD DOG in a pleased tone of voice.

To prevent a puppy from jumping up on people, it must be corrected consistently each time it attempts to do so.

# Collar and
# Leash

We feel it is extremely important that the puppy becomes accustomed to wearing a collar and leash. These two instruments are very valuable. Their function is to provide control over a dog and to keep it from harm's way.

Our puppies are introduced early to a collar and leash. It doesn't take long before they become quite animated at the sight of this equipment. Our dogs know that the collar and leash signify fun times ahead.

The method we use to introduce the collar and leash is as follows:

The puppy is fitted with a training collar that is comfortable. We prefer a lightweight

This is an example of a collar correctly placed
on a dog. Note that the slip ring is attached to
the section of the dog's collar which falls over
the top of the dog's neck.

chain or nylon braided with metal rings. The collar slips easily over the dog's head and ears. After it is on, we reassure the puppy by talking and petting.

The collar is left on the puppy for fifteen minutes two or three times a day; each time the puppy is also reassured. This procedure is repeated until the puppy accepts wearing this new device without fear or resentment. This generally takes only a few days to accomplish.

A collar is used only during the training sessions and for going outside. It is never left on the puppy all the time for safety reasons. A dog could very easily get its collar caught on something, causing injury, even death.

The leash is not introduced to the puppy until it has become accustomed to its collar. We prefer to use leather leashes. The material is durable and easy to handle. The leash is attached to the nonslip ring on the collar. As soon as the leash is put on, the puppy is reassured by talking and petting.

Walking the puppy does not begin yet. The dog must first be allowed to get used to this added device. The procedure for walking is explained in the next section, 'Taking a Walk'.

The leash and collar are kept on the puppy for fifteen minutes, two or three times a day; each time the puppy is also reassured by talking and petting.

If the puppy chooses to walk by itself dragging the leash along, it is allowed to do so if someone is nearby to prevent it from getting tangled. When the puppy is approached in the right manner, it will usually accept wearing this equipment after a few days without showing fear or resentment.

This equipment is used for control and for the safety of the puppy. It is never used to tie the dog to anything, nor is the dog ever hit with a leash!

Any puppy under the age of six months needs no strong leash and collar correction other than a light tug when necessary. This correction is explained in the next section, 'Taking a Walk'. Even after six months of age, a puppy—if it has been correctly handled—should require little or no discipline in this manner.

# Taking a Walk

**Key words:** DOG'S NAME
LET'S GO
GOOD DOG
BACK
OK

**Equipment:** Training collar and leash

As soon as the puppy is accustomed to wearing a collar and an attached leash, it can be taught how to walk keeping pace with the handler.

We believe any puppy should be taught early to walk on a leash in a mannerly fashion. When a dog drags a person down the street, it has to be an exhausting, frustrating and perhaps dangerous experience. Walking with a dog should be a relaxing, pleasant time, not a constant struggle.

Our Doberman Pinschers are rather small as young puppies, however, full grown they are quite large and very strong. It is imperative that we teach our puppies early that we are walking them, not vice versa.

The method we use to teach our puppies to walk properly on a leash is as follows:

The puppy is placed at the handler's left side. The leash is attached to the nonslip ring on the dog's collar. The leash is held in the right hand. The loop handle goes over the right thumb. The leash then falls across the palm and is grasped holding the excess in the hand. Next, it should cross over the front of the handler's body, which helps to control the dog. The leash must be kept with slack in it.

The next step is to motivate the puppy to want to be near the handler. This is accomplished by the handler's tone of voice, along with constant talking. The puppy responds to this. Excited, constant talking teaches a puppy to pay attention to the handler. It also helps to generate the needed enthusiasm a puppy should have so that it will follow alongside happily. To gain the puppy's attention, call it by its NAME, then, with the leash held correctly in the right hand, the puppy at the left

The leash should be attached to the nonslip
ring of the collar.

**The leash should be held in the right hand with the loop handle over the thumb.**

side, the handler says excitedly LET'S GO. At the same time, the handler steps off with the left foot to begin a walk across the room.

When walking it is essential that with each step taken the puppy be coaxed along with enthusiastic, constant talking! Again we remind that this is done to teach a puppy to want to keep its interest focused on the handler.

If the puppy should decide to balk or sit down, stop walking at once. The handler kneels down facing the puppy and begins to coax it in a pleasant, reassuring tone of voice until the puppy responds by going to the handler.

If coaxing does not work, the puppy is **never pulled along by the leash**. The handler goes to the puppy to reassure it by talking and petting. After that, another attempt to walk on leash is begun.

This method, to be effective, is repeated in the same way until the puppy will walk on leash with the handler across the room. The puppy should walk readily and happily alongside the handler, showing neither fear nor resentment. Once this is accomplished, the puppy is taken outside to teach it to walk on leash in a mannerly way.

At first the puppy is carried to an outside location that is relatively quiet, such as the sidewalk of a moderately traveled street. The puppy is held for a few minutes to reassure it about the unfamiliar surroundings. It is gently petted and calmly talked to until it appears comfortable with this new situation. Then the puppy is placed on the ground at the left side of the handler. The leash is held properly in the right hand. The puppy is called by NAME to gain its attention, followed with LET'S GO in an excited tone of voice. At the same time, the handler steps off with the left foot. Immediately the puppy is coaxed along with enthusiastic talking which is constantly done each step along the way!

On the first journey outdoors, the walk is limited to no longer than five to ten minutes. After the first walk outdoors, the length of time is extended and the puppy is exposed to more distracting things, such as heavier traffic or other noises.

Once the puppy will walk happily and readily along without fear or resentment, it is ready to learn the perimeter of a walk. This is done in the following way:

When the puppy starts to become interested in a distraction and begins to lag behind, the handler gives the slack leash a short light tug to regain the puppy's attention. As soon as this is done, the handler coaxes the puppy along with GOOD DOG and enthusiastic encouragement. This procedure is repeated each time the puppy becomes so distracted as to lag behind the handler.

If the puppy starts to forge ahead, the handler says the command BACK, followed by a short quick snap of the slack leash. As soon as the puppy responds by slowing down slightly or turning in the direction of the handler, it is told GOOD DOG in a pleased tone of voice!

This procedure is repeated each time the puppy starts to forge ahead. Command and praise are what we try to accomplish in this exercise to motivate the puppy to enjoy taking walks alongside the handler. At this stage, this is accomplished without the puppy having to learn the formal heel command. By carrying out this training as indicated, the puppy is being taught not to lag whenever it wants to nor to forge ahead. Walks will then be enjoyable and not a constant struggle.

The proper way to begin a walk is with the puppy at the left side. The slack leash must be held correctly in the right hand as the handler steps off on the left foot. The handler must constantly look at and talk to the dog.

Author Ann Brahms is shown with "Meg" the Brahms sixteen week old female Doberman Pinscher puppy.

# Introduction to the Sit / Down / Stand and Recall

**T**he following sections of this book deal with methods of training a puppy to SIT, DOWN, STAND, and RECALL. It is important for the reader to understand that REPETITION is vital in order to teach these exercises. However, excessively long training periods are nonproductive as a puppy is apt to become bored. In order to retain the natural enthusiasm a pet has, limit the training sessions to ten or fifteen minutes each day. DO NOT OVER TRAIN!

Another important point to keep in mind as training begins is that PATIENCE is absolutely necessary. Dogs seldom learn from the first lesson. By carefully following the instructions in the subsequent sections, repeating them over and over again, in the same way each time, the handler will achieve success. One should not lose control of his temper with a puppy. An expression of anger will frighten a pet. This will teach a dog not to trust the handler. A puppy should enjoy training, not fear it. Make training a pleasant, happy experience.

ENTHUSIASM, is a very important ingredient in training dogs. PLEASURE should be expressed with enthusiastic PRAISE each time a puppy follows through correctly, even if it has to be helped to complete an exercise. This coupled with a lot of PETTING is **the only reward** a puppy should come to expect.

Only one member of the household should perform the training. Subtle differences in the way different people carry out the training exercises will tend to confuse a puppy. This will prolong the time required to teach each specific lesson and affect the reliability of the dog. Once a puppy is trained, each member of the family can be taught how to control the dog.

# Sit / Stay

**Key words:** SIT/STAY
GOOD DOG
NO
OK

**Equipment:** Training collar

We train our puppies the SIT / STAY in order to exercise control over them at certain times such as when preparing their meals, in the veterinarian's office and near busy street corners waiting for the traffic to go by.

It became evident to us that the amount of time and effort we spent teaching a puppy to

SIT / STAY was minimal compared with the time wasted trying to control a dog that had not been taught this exercise.

The method we use to teach our dogs the SIT / STAY is as follows:

Kneeling down on the floor beside the puppy, the handler places the puppy in front of him/her; with the right hand, face the puppy to the right by gripping its collar in front, below its head. Place the left hand **palm down** under the puppy's abdomen. If necessary, raise up the left hand just enough to keep the puppy in a standing position. Reassure the dog by talking and petting until it will settle down and stand still. Then move the left hand around behind the puppy, placing it next to the dog's rear, slightly above the hocks. It is very important that the handler **does not** touch the puppy's rear quarters. Next, say the word SIT in a calm but firm tone of voice; it is spoken once and only once! Immediately after the handler says SIT, the puppy is pushed back gently with the right hand, keeping the left hand stationary. The dog moves back slightly, bumping into the left hand. By reflex the puppy will start to move into a sitting position. Continuing to push with the right hand, the handler begins to praise the puppy by saying GOOD DOG as it begins to tuck its rear under. Quickly, but gently, move the left hand to the

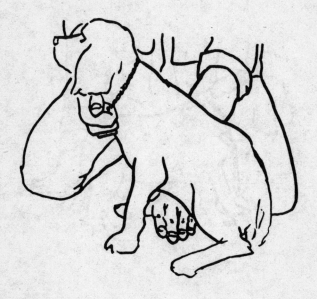

The left hand should be placed palm down
under the puppy's abdomen.

A puppy is placed in the correct position when
it is standing and facing to the right of the
handler. The right hand should grip the dog's
collar below its head. The left hand is placed
behind the puppy next to the dog's rear, but not
touching it. The left hand is held slightly above
the dog's hocks.

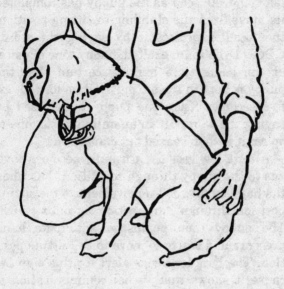

As a puppy begins to tuck its rear under, the left hand is quickly but gently moved to the dog's hips at the base of the tail. The SIT is then completed by applying gentle pressure with the left hand.

dog's hips at the base of the tail; then complete the SIT by applying gentle pressure with the left hand. As soon as the puppy has completed its move from the standing to sitting position, the handler praises it by saying the words GOOD DOG in an excited, happy tone of voice, at the same time making certain that the puppy is kept in the sitting position for at least five seconds. Then the puppy is released by saying the word OK in an enthusiastic tone of voice. It is then coaxed out of position.

After a few lessons, it usually becomes obvious to the puppy through repetition that when the handler says SIT a movement to the sitting position through hand action is coming next. The puppy then begins to anticipate hand pressure and starts to move to the sitting position. The handler keeps alert for this sign because it shows that verbal communication is beginning. Now, instead of continuing to place the left hand behind the dog's hocks, it is moved to the hip area; hand pressure is applied only if necessary to complete the SIT. Again the puppy is praised, as this is the only way it realizes that the handler is pleased with it for responding to the verbal command to SIT.

This exercise is repeated at least ten times in succession every day until the puppy will SIT on command without the benefit of guiding hand pressure.

The next phase of this exercise is designed to teach the puppy to stay in the sitting position until released by the handler. The puppy is given a SIT command, spoken just once! Upon reaching the correct position, the handler holds the right hand about three or four inches in front of the dog's face, much like a stop signal given by crossing guards to halt traffic. This signal is followed by the word STAY, spoken just once in a firm tone of voice.

During the course of this training, a puppy will attempt to get up from the sitting position or lie down before it has been released from doing so. The handler is always prepared for this to happen by responding at once with the word NO, spoken once in a stern tone of voice, while at the same time placing the puppy back into the sitting position.

If the puppy has started to get up, it is returned at once to the sitting position by pressing down gently on its hips with the left hand while the right hand keeps the front of the puppy stationary.

If the puppy starts to lie down, it is returned to the sitting position by pushing up and slightly back with the right hand, while the left hand keeps the dog's rear quarters stationary.

In these situations, after the puppy is returned to the sitting position the word STAY is

## STAY SIGNAL

Upon reaching the correct sitting position, the handler holds the right hand about three or four inches in front of the puppy's face, followed by the word STAY spoken just once in a firm tone of voice.

said once and only once in a firm tone of voice coupled with the hand signal. The count is then resumed for however many seconds the handler intends the exercise to last. Once completed, the puppy is again praised by being told GOOD DOG. Then it is released by saying OK and coaxed out of position.

The length of time that a puppy is required to SIT is increased by five-second intervals until it will sit and stay in this position for at least one minute.

In this exercise—as in all others—the key to success is to be **consistent**. This procedure should be performed the same way every time, saying the same words until the puppy will SIT / STAY on command.

# Down / Stay

**Key words:** DOWN/STAY
NO
GOOD DOG
OK

**Equipment:** Training collar

We teach our puppies to lie down on command in order to eliminate confusion and keep them out of trouble. This is the most comfortable position for a dog to assume; therefore, the DOWN / STAY is used whenever it becomes necessary to keep a dog in one spot for extended periods of time.

The methods we use to teach our puppies this exercise are as follows:

After a puppy has been taught to SIT / STAY, it is placed in that position on the handler's left side, facing forward. Next, the puppy's collar is gripped with the left hand behind its neck, with the left forearm resting on the puppy's back. The right hand is placed behind the puppy's right foreleg. Using the right hand, the handler grips the puppy's left front elbow and says the word DOWN just once in a calm, firm tone of voice. Immediately following this command the right hand is pulled forward while pressing down with the left forearm. The puppy has no choice but to lie down. The moment the puppy is all the way down, it is gently reassured with GOOD DOG. Then the right hand is removed. The left forearm is held in contact with the puppy's back the first few times this exercise is performed. This is done to hold the puppy in the DOWN position. The puppy is held in this position for at least five seconds. The handler then releases the puppy by saying OK just once. The puppy is then coaxed out of position and praised enthusiastically with GOOD DOG!

Within a few days, it should become obvious to the puppy through association and repetition that when the handler says DOWN, a movement to that position will follow. The

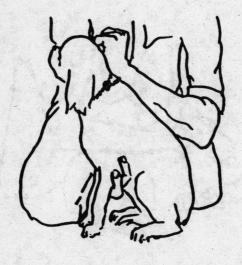

The right hand is pulled forward while pressing
down with the left forearm.

The puppy has no choice but to lie down.

puppy then begins to anticipate hand pressure and starts to go into the DOWN position on its own. At this point, hand pressure is applied **only if necessary** to complete this exercise. Praise is most important at this point because this is how the puppy knows that it has pleased the handler.

This exercise is repeated ten times in succession every day until the puppy will DOWN on command without the need for guiding hand pressure.

The next phase of this exercise is designed to teach the puppy to stay in the DOWN position until released by the handler. The puppy is given a DOWN command, spoken just once! Upon reaching the correct position, the handler holds a hand about three or four inches in front of the dog's face, as outlined in the preceding section on SIT / STAY training. This signal is followed by the word STAY, spoken just once in a firm tone of voice. The handler then silently counts to ten. After this, the puppy is released by saying OK in a pleased tone of voice. Then it is coaxed out of position with enthusiastic praise by saying GOOD DOG! Each time this exercise is performed, the length of time the dog is required to stay DOWN is increased by five seconds. Eventually the puppy will start to rise from the DOWN position. It is crucial that the dog

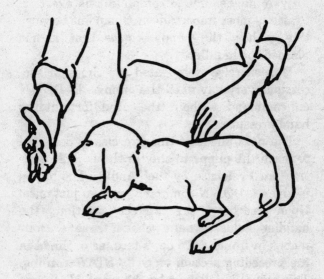

Upon reaching the correct DOWN position, the handler holds a hand three or four inches in front of the puppy's face, followed by the word STAY, spoken just once in a firm tone of voice.

be caught in the act of trying to get up. This is important so that the handler can teach it not to get up until it is released by the word OK. At this moment the puppy is told NO, spoken in a stern tone of voice only once while applying pressure with both hands to the puppy's shoulders and hips to return it to the DOWN position. This is followed by the word STAY, spoken just once in a firm tone of voice! Again, a count is resumed to whatever length of time the handler intends the exercise to last. Finally, the puppy is released by the word OK and coaxed out of position with enthusiastic praise of GOOD DOG!

Each time this exercise is carried out, the length of time is varied so that the puppy doesn't begin to associate a specific time span with the end of the exercise.

The goals of this exercise are for a puppy to DOWN on command and to STAY until released by the word OK. Again, the puppy's only reward is praise which should be lavished in full measure!

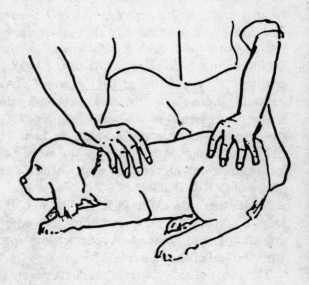

While catching the dog in the act of getting up, the handler says the word NO in a stern tone of voice while applying pressure with both hands to the puppy's shoulders and hips to return it to the DOWN position.

# Stand / Stay

**Key words:** STAND/STAY
NO
EASY
GOOD DOG
OK

**Equipment:** Training collar

The command to STAND / STAY is probably not well known to the average person. However, to people who enter dogs in breed and obedience competition it is commonplace.

People who show dogs in competition must teach their pets to STAND and STAY so that a show judge can examine the anatomy of the dogs. While this is going on, the animals are expected to stay in the position the handlers placed them in until released. They must not shy away or show aggression of any kind.

Our puppies are taught this exercise early, regardless of whether they are going to be

Emery A. Santerre, Jr., D.V.M., Saco, Maine, is shown examining "Meg" at sixteen weeks of age. Author Paul Brahms looks on after he placed Meg in the STAND / STAY position.

shown in competition or not. The reason we
teach it is out of consideration for the veterinarian and her/his staff. The value of this command becomes evident when a vet can
examine a dog that does not move from the position it was placed in until released—showing neither fear nor resentment.

The STAND training is started with the
puppy in the sitting position in front of the
handler, facing to the right. The handler grips
the dog's collar with the right hand under the
chin. The left hand is placed **palm down**
under the puppy's abdomen but **not touching**
it.

The command STAND is given just once in a
firm, calm voice. Immediately following this,
the right hand pulls forward on the collar,
while the left hand is raised **palm down** until
the puppy is standing on all four feet. The instant the dog begins to rise, GOOD DOG is repeated in a pleased tone of voice!

Once the puppy is standing, the right hand
stops pulling but continues to grip the collar to
maintain control. The left hand is lowered to
slightly below the puppy's abdomen; it is still
held palm down, but it no longer touches the
dog. Now the word EASY is repeated in a
calm, reassuring tone of voice. The puppy is
kept in the standing position for at least five

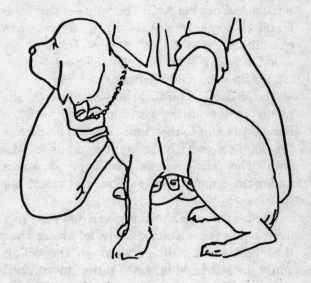

**The left hand should be placed palm down under the puppy's abdomen.**

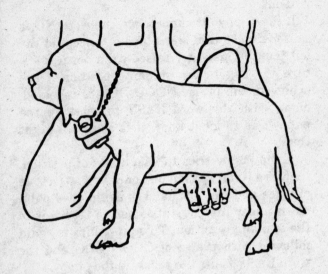

Once the puppy is standing, the right hand stops pulling but continues to grip the collar to maintain control. The left hand is lowered to slightly below the puppy's abdomen; it is still held palm down, but no longer touches the dog.

seconds the first few times this exercise is carried out.

If the puppy attempts to sit, the word NO is said just once in a stern tone of voice and the left hand is instantly raised palm down to return the dog to the standing position. Once achieved, the praise GOOD DOG is repeated, along with the word EASY to reassure the puppy and to let it know it is doing the right thing.

If the puppy tries to wiggle out of position, the word NO is spoken just once in a stern tone of voice and the left hand is again used palm down under the dog's abdomen to return it to the standing position. This procedure is again followed with praise of GOOD DOG and the word EASY is used to reassure the puppy.

Once the puppy has settled down and will remain in the standing position for at least five seconds, it is given the command to SIT, followed by GOOD DOG in a pleased and reassuring tone of voice. This exercise is repeated ten times in succession every day.

Usually, after a few days, most puppies will start to move towards the standing position the moment the left hand, held palm down, starts to touch its abdomen. When this happens, the puppy is beginning to associate the handler's touch with movement toward the standing position. Praise is then lavished to encourage the dog to complete its movement from sitting to standing.

The next sign of achievement is the puppy's response to the command STAND! Through association of voice and hands, the dog will begin to move to the standing position after the command is given in anticipation of the touch of the left hand, palm down, on its abdomen. Guiding hand pressure under the abdomen and pulling on the collar are now kept to a minimum. They are used only if necessary to complete the exercise. Again, words of praise and reassurance are repeated the instant the puppy begins to respond to the command.

Once the puppy will respond to the STAND command—spoken just once—the word STAY is said in a calm, firm voice, the instant the dog is up on all four feet. This command is accompanied by the hand signal for stay. The left hand is now used to gently stroke the puppy's back, while saying "EASY" to reassure it. Increase the length of time the puppy is required to STAY in this position by five-second increments untill it will STAND / STAY for one full minute.

At this point, the handler keeps alert for movement of the feet. The instant the puppy starts to move out of the specific position it assumed, the handler quickly, but gently, places

Once the puppy will respond to the STAND command—spoken just once—the word STAY is said in a calm, firm voice, the instant the dog is up on all four feet. This command is accompanied by the hand signal for stay.

the left hand palm down under the dog's abdomen. This is followed with the word NO said once in a calm, stern voice while raising the left hand palm down so that it touches the puppy's abdomen. At the same time the right hand pulls forward on the collar. This is followed by the word STAY, used once! At this point the right hand stops pulling forward but continues to grip the collar to maintain needed control. The left hand is once again used to gently stroke the puppy's back, while reassuring it with the word EASY.

After the puppy will STAND and STAY for one full minute without moving out of position, the exercise is carried out with a family member or friend approaching the puppy from the front while it is on the STAND / STAY exercise. No words are spoken by the person who approaches the puppy. The procedure is to go calmly up to the dog with the left hand extended downward to allow the puppy to sniff the back of the hand. This is to allow the puppy to become comfortable with the person. After that, the person walks on by. This is all that is necessary the first few times. If the puppy should attempt to move, the same procedure is carried out as previously outlined to return the dog to the STAND / STAY position.

Once the puppy will STAND and STAY with the approach of a familiar person, it is now ready to experience a simulated vet's examination. The person approaches the puppy, again from the front, and lets it sniff the back of the hand. Next, while walking alongside the puppy the person gently runs the left hand across the top of its back, just one time. Hand contact is increased after a puppy will STAND and STAY without moving out of position until released. At that time, a familiar person should be able to approach and examine the entire anatomy of the puppy without a struggle.

This exercise is carried out with as many different people as possible until the puppy has learned to STAND and STAY while a perfect stranger examines the dog and it shows no shyness, resentment or inclination to move out of position.

# Recall

**Key words:** DOG'S NAME
COME
GOOD DOG

**Equipment:** Training collar / leash / clothesline

Recently, one of the most pathetic examples of the value of RECALL happened to a friend who was walking his dog, off leash, on a quiet country road. The sound of a car could be heard rounding the curve ahead. At just that moment, a ground squirrel rustling in leaves across the road caught the dog's attention. The dog eagerly raced toward the squirrel.

# Recall

Our friend called to his pet to come back to him, but as always, if something more exciting was happening than returning to its master, it generally chose to ignore the call.

Suddenly all that could be heard was the sound of high-pitched screeching tires, then a terrible thud as the bumper of a car slammed into the dog, crushing its rib cage. Both front and rear wheels then ran over the dog.

The pain must have been excruciating but with the last remaining strength it had, the dog crawled back across the road to within inches of its now horrified master and died. It had returned to its master but it was too late.

Countless dogs are killed, maimed or lost each year because they were not taught by their masters to return to them when called.

This is one exercise we insist our dogs learn for obvious reasons. A puppy should be taught to RECALL **after** it knows its name and has had the benefit of having been taught the lesson outlined earlier, 'Taking a Walk'.

The procedure we use for the RECALL is as follows:

A routine walk is started with the leash attached to the slip ring on the dog's collar. As soon as the puppy begins to focus its attention on a distraction, the handler backs up two or three short steps, calls the puppy by NAME, followed by the command COME in a firm, ex-

**The leash is attached to the slip ring on dog's collar.**

As soon as the puppy begins to focus its attention on a distraction, the handler backs up two or three short steps and calls the puppy by name. She/he follows with the command COME in a firm, excited tone of voice. Immediately after this, the leash is given a short quick jerk.

cited tone of voice. The DOG'S NAME and COME are spoken once and only once! Immediately after this, the leash is given a short quick jerk. The purpose of this is to lightly jolt the puppy's attention away from the distraction. The instant the puppy turns in the direction of the voice and the jerk, the handler begins to praise and coax the dog to return. This must be done in a happy, excited tone of voice.

This procedure is repeated daily for a period of at least one week. Since the purpose of this method is to develop a reliable RECALL, the puppy is not called to return to the handler every time it becomes interested in a distraction. Instead, the procedure is carried out every second or third time the puppy's attention becomes intensely focused on something other than the handler. Done in this way, the dog is allowed to enjoy some freedom to look at the world. The puppy soon learns that when its NAME is called, followed by the command COME, said once and only once, it had better forget any distractions and head back to the handler or a jerk on the leash will follow.

Once a puppy will respond immediately to the command COME without the handler having to jerk the leash, we feel the dog is ready for the next phase of training. A fifteen-foot nylon clothesline is attached to the slip ring of the collar and the puppy is taken to an area that is filled with exciting new distractions. The handler allows the puppy to amble on ahead until it becomes thoroughly engrossed in a distraction and starts to run toward it. At this time the handler stops abruptly, calls the DOG'S NAME followed by the command COME in a loud, clear voice, spoken once and only once! This is the ultimate test, for if the puppy has learned to RECALL when it is intently running toward something exciting, it will stop and return immediately to the handler, whereupon it is lavished with happy, enthusiastic praise.

If the puppy chooses to ignore the RECALL, the clothesline is held tightly with both hands. In short order the dog will reach the end of the line with considerable force. If done properly, this causes the dog to be stopped short, flipped into the air and dropped to the ground. The handler remains at the spot from where the puppy was called and begins to coax its return with words of consolation such as "You poor thing!" "What happened to you?" "Good dog!" etc., until the puppy is in the handler's arms being showered with attention.

This exercise is repeated possibly one or two times. However, most puppies learn this lesson very quickly and will RECALL after the second time.

## Recall

As in all training, reinforcement is needed on occasion so that the puppy will perform the RECALL reliably. We repeat this procedure for two weeks, every two or three days. At the end of this time, every puppy of ours has responded to the RECALL immediately, regardless of the distractions.

# Things to Remember

- Be certain to always praise your puppy when it does something to please you. Use a happy tone of voice. Be extra enthusiastic for your joy will be the pup's only reward.

- When a puppy makes a mistake, use a firm, displeased tone of voice. The dog will understand from this that you are displeased with its actions.

- A dog that responds to the first COMMAND is well trained. Repetition of a command teaches a puppy that it can disregard authority. Disobedience will be the end result.

- Make training a pleasant experience, a really happy time. A puppy will respond much better to being taught if the handler is enthusiastic.

- Do not call a dog to you for punishment. If you do, you will teach it that returning is a time for discipline, and he probably will not come back.

- Never keep a collar on a dog all the time. It could be very dangerous. A puppy may get a collar caught on something, causing injury, even death. Use a collar for training lessons and taking walks.

## Things to Remember

- Timing is critical in training a dog, both in making corrections and giving praise.

- Never use an object of any kind to correct your pet. Remember, your voice is all you need to let a puppy know that you are displeased.

- Do not lose your temper while training your puppy. You will teach the puppy not to trust you and not to enjoy your companionship.

- Always be consistent in your training. Train every day, in the same way.

# The Crate

Often it is useful to confine your puppy to a safe area where he/she will be unable to get into mischief in your absence. This is particularly useful as sleeping quarters for puppies during housebreaking training. Started early the puppy will view the area as a refuge.

We use the portable metal crates which can be transported easily in the trunk of a car or in the rear of a station wagon. On trips this affords our dogs a familiar place in which to rest regardless of where we travel.

# A Final Word to the Puppy Owner

If you've found the wording in this book to be repetitious, then congratulations! You've discovered the key to successfully training your puppy. The instructions you give to your puppy must be clear, concise and consistent. Your puppy wants to please you and do what you want. Once you've learned these simple rules of communication, you and your puppy will soon be speaking the same language.

# About the Authors

Ann and Paul Brahms bred and taught obedience and breed-handling classes for several years. They live in Portland, Maine, with their five children. Paul Brahms, Jr., who illustrated the book, is a recent graduate of the Rhode Island School of Design.